ANGELIS
PUBLICATIONS

ISBN: 978-0-9956949-5-8
Published by Angelis Publications
www.angelispublications.com
Cover Design © Angie J Anderson

Welcome

_____

_____

_____

_____

_____

_____

_____

_____

_____

_____

Will you please allow us to share your testimonial? If so please ✓ or ✗ the box Thanks!

Name & We're From .....   **Comments**

		☐
		☐
		☐
		☐

Will you please allow us to share your testimonial? If so please ✓ *or* ✗ *the* box *Thanks!*

Name & We're From .....   **Comments**

Will you please allow us to share your testimonial? If so please ✔ or ✘ the |box| Thanks!

Name & We're From .....   **Comments**

Will you please allow us to share your testimonial? If so please ✓ or ✗ the | box | Thanks!

Name & We're From .....   Comments

		☐
		☐
		☐
		☐

Will you please allow us to share your testimonial? If so please ✓ or ✗ the ⬚box⬚ *Thanks!*

Name & We're From .....   **Comments**

		☐
		☐
		☐
		☐

Will you please allow us to share your testimonial? If so please ✓ or ✗ the ☐box☐ Thanks!

Name & We're From .....   **Comments**

Name & We're From	Comments	
		☐
		☐
		☐
		☐

Will you please allow us to share your testimonial? If so please ✓ *or* ✗ *the* | box | *Thanks!*

Name & We're From .....   **Comments**

Will you please allow us to share your testimonial? If so please ✓ or ✗ the box Thanks!

Name & We're From .....   **Comments**

Name & We're From	Comments	
		☐
		☐
		☐
		☐

Will you please allow us to share your testimonial? If so please ✓ *or* ✗ *the* box *Thanks!*

Name & We're From .....   **Comments**

Name & We're From	Comments	
		☐
		☐
		☐
		☐

Will you please allow us to share your testimonial? If so please ✓ or ✗ the │box│ Thanks!

Name & We're From .....   **Comments**

Will you please allow us to share your testimonial? If so please ✓ *or* ✗ *the* | box | *Thanks!*

Name & We're From .....   **Comments**

Will you please allow us to share your testimonial? If so please ✓ or ✗ the ⬚box⬚ Thanks!

Name & We're From	Comments	
		⬚
		⬚
		⬚
		⬚

Will you please allow us to share your testimonial? If so please ✓ or ✗ the box Thanks!

Name & We're From .....   **Comments**

Name & We're From	Comments	

Will you please allow us to share your testimonial? If so please ✓ or ✗ the ⬛box Thanks!

Name & We're From .....   **Comments**

Will you please allow us to share your testimonial? If so please ✓ or ✗ the box Thanks!

Name & We're From .....   **Comments**

Will you please allow us to share your testimonial? If so please ✓ or ✗ the ☐ box Thanks!

Name & We're From .....   **Comments**

Will you please allow us to share your testimonial? If so please ✓ or ✗ the │box│ Thanks!

Name & We're From .....   **Comments**

Will you please allow us to share your testimonial? If so please ✓ or ✗ the box *Thanks!*

Name & We're From .....   **Comments**

Will you please allow us to share your testimonial? If so please ✓ or ✗ the box Thanks!

Name & We're From .....   **Comments**

Will you please allow us to share your testimonial? If so please ✓ or ✗ the box *Thanks!*

Name & We're From .....   Comments

Will you please allow us to share your testimonial? If so please ✓ or ✗ the [box] Thanks!

Name & We're From .....   **Comments**

Name & We're From	Comments	

Will you please allow us to share your testimonial? If so please ✓ or ✗ the | box | *Thanks!*

Name & We're From .....   **Comments**

Will you please allow us to share your testimonial? If so please ✓ or ✗ the | box | *Thanks!*

Name & We're From .....   **Comments**

Will you please allow us to share your testimonial? If so please ✓ *or* ✗ *the* | box | *Thanks!*

Name & We're From .....   Comments

Will you please allow us to share your testimonial? If so please ✓ or ✗ the │box│ Thanks!

Name & We're From .....   **Comments**

		☐
		☐
		☐
		☐

Will you please allow us to share your testimonial? If so please ✓ or ✗ the [box] Thanks!

Name & We're From .....   Comments

Will you please allow us to share your testimonial? If so please ✓ or ✗ the ☐box Thanks!

Name & We're From .....   **Comments**

Will you please allow us to share your testimonial? If so please ✓ or ✗ the box Thanks!

Name & We're From .....   **Comments**

Will you please allow us to share your testimonial? If so please ✓ or ✗ the ⬚box⬚ *Thanks!*

Name & We're From .....   **Comments**

Name & We're From	Comments	
		⬚
		⬚
		⬚
		⬚

Will you please allow us to share your testimonial? If so please ✓ or ✗ the box Thanks!

Name & We're From .....   **Comments**

		□
		□
		□
		□

Will you please allow us to share your testimonial? If so please ✓ or ✗ the box Thanks!

Name & We're From .....   **Comments**

Will you please allow us to share your testimonial? If so please ✓ or ✗ the [box] Thanks!

Name & We're From .....   **Comments**

Will you please allow us to share your testimonial? If so please ✓ *or* ✗ *the* [box] *Thanks!*

Name & We're From .....   **Comments**

		☐
		☐
		☐
		☐

Will you please allow us to share your testimonial? If so please ✓ or ✗ the │box│ Thanks!

Name & We're From .....   **Comments**

Name & We're From	Comments	

Will you please allow us to share your testimonial? If so please ✓ or ✗ the box Thanks!

Name & We're From .....   **Comments**

Will you please allow us to share your testimonial? If so please ✓ *or* ✗ *the* | box | *Thanks!*

Name & We're From .....   **Comments**

Will you please allow us to share your testimonial? If so please ✓ or ✗ the box Thanks!

Name & We're From .....   **Comments**

Will you please allow us to share your testimonial? If so please ✓ or ✗ the │box│ Thanks!

Name & We're From .....   Comments

Name & We're From	Comments	

Will you please allow us to share your testimonial? If so please ✓ or ✗ the box *Thanks!*

Name & We're From .....   **Comments**

Will you please allow us to share your testimonial? If so please ✓ or ✗ the [box] Thanks!

Name & We're From .....   Comments

Name & We're From	Comments	
		☐
		☐
		☐
		☐

Will you please allow us to share your testimonial? If so please ✓ or ✗ the [box] Thanks!

Name & We're From .....   **Comments**

Will you please allow us to share your testimonial? If so please ✓ or ✗ the | box | *Thanks!*

Name & We're From .....   **Comments**

Will you please allow us to share your testimonial? If so please ✓ *or* ✗ *the* | box | *Thanks!*

Name & We're From .....   **Comments**

Will you please allow us to share your testimonial? If so please ✓ or ✗ the box Thanks!

Name & We're From .....   Comments

Will you please allow us to share your testimonial? If so please ✓ or ✗ the box Thanks!

Name & We're From .....   **Comments**

Will you please allow us to share your testimonial? If so please ✓ or ✗ the |box| Thanks!

Name & We're From .....   Comments

Name & We're From	Comments	
		☐
		☐
		☐
		☐

Will you please allow us to share your testimonial? If so please ✓ or ✗ the │box│ Thanks!

Name & We're From .....   **Comments**

		☐
		☐
		☐
		☐

Will you please allow us to share your testimonial? If so please ✓ or ✗ the box Thanks!

Name & We're From .....   Comments

		☐
		☐
		☐
		☐

Will you please allow us to share your testimonial? If so please ✓ or ✗ the [box] Thanks!

Name & We're From ..... Comments

Name & We're From	Comments	
		☐
		☐
		☐
		☐

Will you please allow us to share your testimonial? If so please ✓ or ✗ the [box] Thanks!

Name & We're From .....   **Comments**

Name & We're From	Comments	
		☐
		☐
		☐
		☐

Will you please allow us to share your testimonial? If so please ✓ *or* ✗ *the* [box] *Thanks!*

Name & We're From .....   **Comments**

		☐
		☐
		☐
		☐

Will you please allow us to share your testimonial? If so please ✓ or ✗ the |box| Thanks!

Name & We're From .....

Comments

		☐
		☐
		☐
		☐

Will you please allow us to share your testimonial? If so please ✓ or ✗ the box Thanks!

Name & We're From .....   **Comments**

		☐
		☐
		☐
		☐

Will you please allow us to share your testimonial? If so please ✓ or ✗ the box Thanks!

Name & We're From .....   **Comments**

Will you please allow us to share your testimonial? If so please ✓ *or* ✗ *the* box *Thanks!*

Name & We're From .....   **Comments**

		☐
		☐
		☐
		☐

Will you please allow us to share your testimonial? If so please ✓ or ✗ the box Thanks!

Name & We're From .....   **Comments**

Will you please allow us to share your testimonial? If so please ✓ or ✗ the box Thanks!

Name & We're From .....   **Comments**

Will you please allow us to share your testimonial? If so please ✓ or ✗ the box Thanks!

Name & We're From .....   Comments

Will you please allow us to share your testimonial? If so please ✓ or ✗ the box Thanks.

Name & We're From .....   **Comments**

		☐
		☐
		☐
		☐

Will you please allow us to share your testimonial? If so please ✓ or ✗ the |box| Thanks!

Name & We're From .....   Comments

Will you please allow us to share your testimonial? If so please ✓ or ✗ the box Thanks!

Name & We're From .....   **Comments**

Will you please allow us to share your testimonial? If so please ✓ or ✗ the box Thanks!

Name & We're From .....   **Comments**

Name & We're From	Comments	

Will you please allow us to share your testimonial? If so please ✓ or ✗ the box Thanks!

Name & We're From .....   **Comments**

Will you please allow us to share your testimonial? If so please ✓ or ✗ the box Thanks!

Name & We're From .....   **Comments**

Will you please allow us to share your testimonial? If so please ✓ *or* ✗ *the* | box | *Thanks!*

Name & We're From .....   **Comments**

		☐
		☐
		☐
		☐

Will you please allow us to share your testimonial? If so please ✓ or ✗ the box Thanks!

Name & We're From .....   Comments

Will you please allow us to share your testimonial? If so please ✓ or ✗ the box Thanks!

Name & We're From .....   **Comments**

Name & We're From	Comments	
		☐
		☐
		☐
		☐

Will you please allow us to share your testimonial? If so please ✓ or ✗ the box *Thanks!*

Name & We're From .....   **Comments**

Name & We're From	Comments	

Will you please allow us to share your testimonial? If so please ✓ *or* ✗ *the* ⬚box⬚ *Thanks!*

Name & We're From .....   **Comments**

		⬚
		⬚
		⬚
		⬚

Will you please allow us to share your testimonial? If so please ✓ or ✗ the box Thanks!

Name & We're From .....   Comments

Will you please allow us to share your testimonial? If so please ✓ or ✗ the | box | *Thanks!*

Name & We're From .....   **Comments**

Will you please allow us to share your testimonial? If so please ✓ or ✗ the box Thanks!

Name & We're From .....   Comments

Name & We're From	Comments	
		☐
		☐
		☐
		☐

Will you please allow us to share your testimonial? If so please ✓ or ✗ the [box] Thanks!

Name & We're From .....   **Comments**

Name & We're From	Comments	
		☐
		☐
		☐
		☐

Will you please allow us to share your testimonial? If so please ✓ or ✗ the box Thanks!

Name & We're From .....   **Comments**

Will you please allow us to share your testimonial? If so please ✓ or ✗ the box Thanks!

Name & We're From .....   **Comments**

Name & We're From	Comments	
		☐
		☐
		☐
		☐

Will you please allow us to share your testimonial? If so please ✓ or ✗ the box Thanks!

Name & We're From .....   Comments

Will you please allow us to share your testimonial? If so please ✓ or ✗ the [box] Thanks!

Name & We're From .....   **Comments**

Will you please allow us to share your testimonial? If so please ✓ or ✗ the [box] Thanks!

Name & We're From .....   **Comments**

		☐
		☐
		☐
		☐

Will you please allow us to share your testimonial? If so please ✓ or ✗ the box Thanks!

Name & We're From .....   **Comments**

Will you please allow us to share your testimonial? If so please ✓ or ✗ the | box | Thanks!

Name & We're From .....   **Comments**

Will you please allow us to share your testimonial? If so please ✓ *or* ✗ *the* box *Thanks!*

Name & We're From .....   **Comments**

		☐
		☐
		☐
		☐

Will you please allow us to share your testimonial? *If so please* ✓ *or* ✗ *the* │box│ *Thanks!*

Name & We're From .....   **Comments**

Will you please allow us to share your testimonial? If so please ✓ or ✗ the box Thanks!

Name & We're From .....   **Comments**

Will you please allow us to share your testimonial? If so please ✓ or ✗ the box Thanks!

Name & We're From .....   Comments

Will you please allow us to share your testimonial? If so please ✓ or ✗ the box Thanks!

Name & We're From .....   **Comments**

		☐
		☐
		☐
		☐

Will you please allow us to share your testimonial? If so please ✓ or ✗ the box Thanks!

Name & We're From .....   **Comments**

Name & We're From	Comments	

Will you please allow us to share your testimonial? If so please ✓ or ✗ the │box│ Thanks!

Name & We're From .....   **Comments**

Will you please allow us to share your testimonial? If so please ✓ or ✗ the box Thanks!

Name & We're From .....   Comments

Name & We're From	Comments	

Will you please allow us to share your testimonial? If so please ✓ or ✗ the box Thanks!

Name & We're From .....   **Comments**

Will you please allow us to share your testimonial? If so please ✓ or ✗ the box Thanks!

Name & We're From .....   Comments

Will you please allow us to share your testimonial? If so please ✓ *or* ✗ *the* box *Thanks!*

Name & We're From .....   **Comments**

Will you please allow us to share your testimonial? If so please ✓ or ✗ the [box] Thanks!

Name & We're From .....   **Comments**

Will you please allow us to share your testimonial? If so please ✓ or ✗ the box Thanks!

Name & We're From .....   **Comments**

Will you please allow us to share your testimonial? If so please ✓ or ✗ the box Thanks!

Name & We're From .....   Comments

		☐
		☐
		☐
		☐

Will you please allow us to share your testimonial? If so please ✓ or ✗ the box *Thanks!*

Name & We're From .....   **Comments**

Name & We're From	Comments	

Will you please allow us to share your testimonial? If so please ✓ *or* ✗ *the* |box| *Thanks!*

Name & We're From .....   **Comments**

		☐
		☐
		☐
		☐

www.ingramcontent.com/pod-product-compliance
Lightning Source LLC
Chambersburg PA
CBHW080148310326
41914CB00090B/896